3 Ingredient Recipes

Starts & Sips   2

Beef & Pork   18

Poultry & Seafood   38

Simple Sides   56

Lots of Sweets   76

Acknowledgments   94

Index   95

Starts & Sips

Crispy Bacon Sticks

½ cup (1½ ounces) grated Wisconsin Parmesan
  cheese, divided
5 slices bacon, halved lengthwise
10 breadsticks

MICROWAVE DIRECTIONS

Spread ¼ cup cheese on plate. Press one side of bacon into cheese; wrap diagonally around breadstick with cheese-coated side toward stick. Place on paper plate or microwave-safe baking sheet lined with paper towels. Repeat with remaining bacon halves, cheese and breadsticks. Microwave on HIGH 4 to 6 minutes until bacon is cooked, checking for doneness after 4 minutes. Roll again in remaining ¼ cup Parmesan cheese. Serve warm. *Makes 10 sticks*

Favorite recipe from *Wisconsin Milk Marketing Board*

Original Ranch® Drummettes

**1 packet (1 ounce) HIDDEN VALLEY® The Original
Ranch® Salad Dressing & Seasoning Mix
¼ cup vegetable oil
24 chicken drummettes (about 2 pounds)**

Combine dressing mix and oil in large bowl. Add drummettes;
toss well to coat. Arrange on rack placed in foil-lined baking
pan; bake at 425°F for 25 minutes. Turn drummettes over; bake
additional 20 minutes.   *Makes 24 drummettes*

*Spicy Hot Variation: Add 2 tablespoons red pepper sauce to dressing
mixture before coating.*

*Serving Suggestion: Dip cooked drummettes in prepared
Hidden Valley® Original Ranch® salad dressing.*

Chocolate-Blueberry Soy Shake

**5 ounces (½ cup plus 2 tablespoons) soymilk
2 tablespoons frozen or fresh blueberries
(about 20 berries)
¼ teaspoon unsweetened cocoa powder
¼ cup crushed ice**

Place all ingredients in blender; blend at high speed 30 seconds
or until well blended. Pour into chilled glass to serve.

Makes 1 serving

Egg Cream

½ cup half-and-half, divided
2 tablespoons chocolate syrup, divided
2 cups unsweetened seltzer water or club soda,
chilled and divided

Pour ¼ cup half-and-half into each of two tall glasses; stir
1 tablespoon chocolate syrup into each. Add 1 cup seltzer
to each glass. *Makes 2 servings*

Holiday Meatballs

1 package Original or Italian Style Meatballs
1 cup HEINZ® Chili Sauce
1 cup grape jelly

Heat meatballs according to package directions. Meanwhile, in
small saucepan, combine chili sauce and grape jelly. Heat until
jelly is melted. Place meatballs in serving dish. Pour chili sauce
mixture over meatballs; stir gently to coat. Serve warm.
Makes 60 appetizers

Tip: *For a zestier sauce, substitute hot jalapeño jelly for grape jelly.*

Perfectly Seasoned Popcorn

2 quarts (8 cups) popped popcorn
1 teaspoon (or to taste) LAWRY'S® Seasoned Salt
Unsalted butter, melted (optional)

In large bowl, toss popcorn and Seasoned Salt together. If
desired, toss with melted butter, to taste.
Makes about 2 servings

Prep Time: 2 to 3 minutes

Fast Pesto Focaccia

1 can (10 ounces) refrigerated pizza crust dough
2 tablespoons prepared pesto
4 sun-dried tomatoes (packed in oil), drained

1. Preheat oven to 425°F. Lightly grease 8-inch square baking pan. Unroll pizza dough. Fold in half; press gently into pan.

2. Spread pesto evenly over dough. Chop tomatoes or snip with kitchen scissors; sprinkle over pesto. Press tomatoes into dough. Using wooden spoon handle, make indentations in dough every 2 inches.

3. Bake 10 to 12 minutes or until golden brown. Cut into 16 squares. Serve warm or at room temperature.

Makes 16 servings

Prep and Cook Time: 20 minutes

Strawberry-Banana Yogurt Energy Drink

1 box (10 ounces) BIRDS EYE® frozen Strawberries, partially thawed
2 medium bananas
¾ cup plain yogurt

• Place all ingredients in blender or food processor; blend until smooth.

Makes 2½ cups

Serving Suggestion: *Add 2 teaspoons wheat germ or ¼ cup fruit juice.*

Prep Time: 5 minutes

Cherry Chocolate Frosty

1 container (6 ounces) chocolate yogurt
½ cup frozen dark sweet cherries
⅛ to ¼ teaspoon almond extract

Combine all ingredients in blender. Cover; blend on high speed 15 to 30 seconds or until smooth. Pour into glass; serve immediately.

Makes 1 serving

Roasted Red Pepper Dip

1 envelope LIPTON® RECIPE SECRETS® Onion Soup Mix
1 container (16 ounces) regular sour cream
1 jar (7 ounces) roasted red peppers, drained and chopped

1. In large bowl, combine all ingredients; chill, if desired.

2. Serve, if desired, with bread sticks, celery or carrot sticks, cooked tortellini or mozzarella sticks.

Makes 2 cups dip

Zesty Blue Cheese Dip

½ cup blue cheese salad dressing
¼ cup sour cream
2 teaspoons *Frank's*® *RedHot*® Original Cayenne Pepper Sauce

Combine all ingredients in medium serving bowl; mix well. Garnish with crumbled blue cheese, if desired.

Makes ¾ cup dip

Prep Time: 5 minutes

Baked Brie

½ pound Brie cheese, rind removed
¼ cup chopped pecans
¼ cup KARO® Dark Corn Syrup

1. Preheat oven to 350°F. Place cheese in shallow oven-safe serving dish. Top with pecans and corn syrup.

2. Bake 8 to 10 minutes or until cheese is almost melted. Serve warm with plain crackers or melba toast.   *Makes 8 servings*

Prep Time: 3 minutes
Cook Time: 10 minutes

Salsa Onion Dip

1 envelope LIPTON® RECIPE SECRETS® Onion
   Soup Mix
1 container (16 ounces) sour cream
½ cup salsa

1. In medium bowl, combine all ingredients; chill, if desired.

2. Serve with your favorite dippers.   *Makes 2½ cups dip*

Prep Time: 5 minutes

Baked Brie

Frozen Watermelon Whip

1¾ cups ice
1 cup coarsely chopped seedless watermelon
**1 cup brewed lemon-flavored herbal tea, at
  room temperature**

Combine all ingredients in blender container. Cover; blend on
high speed until smooth, pulsing to break up all ice. Pour into
2 tall glasses; serve immediately.   *Makes 2 servings*

Crabmeat Spread

1 package (8 ounces) cream cheese, softened
¼ cup cocktail sauce
1 package (8 ounces) imitation crabmeat

1. Spread cream cheese evenly on serving plate. Pour cocktail
sauce over cream cheese; top with imitation crabmeat.

2. Serve with cocktail rye bread or assorted crackers.
                                      Makes 1½ cups spread

Vegetable Cream Cheese

**1 envelope LIPTON® RECIPE SECRETS® Vegetable
  Soup Mix**
**2 packages (8 ounces each) cream cheese,
  softened**
2 tablespoons milk

1. In medium bowl, combine all ingredients; chill 2 hours.

2. Serve on bagels or with assorted fresh vegetables.
                                      Makes 2½ cups spread

Prep Time: 10 minutes
Chill Time: 2 hours

Bandito Buffalo Wings

**1 package (1.25 ounces) ORTEGA® Taco
    Seasoning Mix
12 (about 1 pound *total*) chicken wings
    ORTEGA Salsa (any flavor)**

PREHEAT oven to 375°F. Lightly grease 13×9-inch baking pan.

PLACE seasoning mix in heavy-duty plastic or paper bag. Add
3 chicken wings; shake well to coat. Place wings in prepared
pan. Repeat until all wings have been coated.

BAKE for 35 to 40 minutes or until juices run clear. Serve with
salsa for dipping. *Makes 6 appetizer servings*

Orange Smoothies

**1 cup vanilla ice cream or vanilla frozen yogurt
¾ cup milk
¼ cup frozen orange juice concentrate**

1. Combine ice cream, milk and orange juice concentrate in
food processor or blender. Cover; blend on high until smooth.

2. Pour mixture into 2 glasses; garnish as desired. Serve
immediately. *Makes 2 servings*

Beef & Pork

Cranberry-Onion Pork Roast

1 boneless pork loin roast (about 2 pounds)
1 can (16 ounces) whole cranberry sauce
1 package (1 ounce) dry onion soup mix

Season roast with salt and pepper; place over indirect heat on grill. Stir together cranberry sauce and onion soup mix in small microwavable bowl. Heat, covered, in microwave until hot, about 1 minute. Baste roast with cranberry mixture every 10 minutes until roast is done (internal temperature with a meat thermometer is 155° to 160°F), about 30 to 45 minutes. Let roast rest about 5 to 8 minutes before slicing to serve. Heat any leftover basting mixture to boiling; stir and boil for 5 minutes. Serve alongside roast. *Makes 4 to 6 servings*

Favorite recipe from **National Pork Board**

Slow Cooker Mesquite Beef

1 boneless beef chuck roast (about 4 to
   5 pounds)
1 cup LAWRY'S® Mesquite Marinade, divided
   French rolls, flour tortillas or taco shells
   (optional)

SLOW COOKER DIRECTIONS

Trim fat from meat. Place meat in slow cooker. Pour ¾ cup
Mesquite Marinade over meat. Cover and cook on LOW for
9 to 10 hours. Remove meat to platter and shred with fork.
Return meat to slow cooker with juices; add remaining ¼ cup
Mesquite Marinade. Serve shredded beef in warmed French
rolls, warmed flour tortillas or taco shells, if desired.

Makes 8 to 10 servings (or two meals of 4 to 5 servings each)

Meal Idea: *Add your favorite frozen stew vegetables during the last
hour of cooking for a pot roast/stew meal.*

Prep Time: 3 to 4 minutes
Slow Cooker Time: 9 to 10 hours

Mama's Easy Awesome Meat Sauce

1 pound ground beef
1 large onion, thinly sliced
1 jar (1 pound 10 ounces) RAGÚ® ROBUSTO!®
   Pasta Sauce

In 12-inch nonstick skillet, brown ground beef with onion;
drain, if desired.

Stir in Pasta Sauce and bring to a boil. Reduce heat to low
and simmer covered, stirring occasionally, 5 minutes. Serve,
if desired, over your favorite hot pasta.   *Makes 4 servings*

Prep Time: 5 minutes
Cook Time: 10 minutes

Dizzy Dogs

**1 package (11 ounces) refrigerated
breadstick dough (12 count)
12 hot dogs
1 egg white**

1. Preheat oven to 375°F.

2. Wrap each hot dog with 1 piece of breadstick dough in spiral pattern. Brush breadstick dough with egg white. Sprinkle with sesame seeds or poppy seeds, if desired. Place on ungreased baking sheet.

3. Bake 12 to 15 minutes or until light golden brown. Serve with condiments for dipping, if desired.   *Makes 12 servings*

Grilled Smoked Sausage

**1 cup apricot or pineapple preserves
1 tablespoon lemon juice
1½ pounds smoked sausage**

Heat preserves in small saucepan until melted. Strain; reserve fruit pieces for another use. Combine strained preserve liquid with lemon juice in a small bowl to make glaze.

Oil hot grid to help prevent sticking. Grill whole sausage on an uncovered grill, over low KINGSFORD® Briquets, 10 minutes. Halfway through cooking, baste with glaze, then turn and continue grilling until heated through. Remove sausage from grill; baste with glaze.   *Makes 4 to 5 servings*

Beef & Pork

Lipton® Onion Burgers

**1 envelope LIPTON® RECIPE SECRETS® Onion
Soup Mix***
2 pounds ground beef
½ cup water

**Also terrific with LIPTON® RECIPE SECRETS® Beefy Onion, Onion
Mushroom, Beefy Mushroom, Savory Herb with Garlic or Ranch Soup Mix.*

1. In large bowl, combine all ingredients; shape into 8 patties.

2. Grill or broil until done. *Makes 8 servings*

Prep Time: 10 minutes
Cook Time: 12 minutes

Fantastic Pot Roast

2½ pounds boneless beef chuck roast
1 can (12 ounces) cola
1 bottle (10 ounces) chili sauce

SLOW COOKER DIRECTIONS

1. Combine all ingredients in slow cooker.

2. Cover; cook on LOW 6 to 8 hours. *Makes 6 servings*

Easy Beef Sandwiches

1 large onion, sliced
1 boneless beef bottom round roast
    (about 3 to 5 pounds)
1 package (1 ounce) au jus gravy mix

SLOW COOKER DIRECTIONS

1. Place onion slices in bottom of slow cooker; top with roast. Combine 1 cup water and au jus mix in small bowl; pour over roast.

2. Cover; cook on LOW 7 to 9 hours. Shred beef; serve on sandwich rolls.   *Makes 6 to 8 servings*

Maple-Glazed Ham

4 slices ham (3 ounces each)
¼ cup maple syrup
1 teaspoon Dijon mustard

1. Preheat broiler.

2. Place ham slices on broiler pan. Combine syrup and mustard in small bowl. Brush each slice with about 1½ teaspoons of syrup mixture.

3. Broil 4 inches below heat about 4 minutes or until ham starts to brown. Turn and brush with remaining syrup mixture. Broil until browned.   *Makes 4 servings*

BBQ Roast Beef

2 pounds boneless cooked roast beef
1 bottle (12 ounces) barbecue sauce
10 to 12 sandwich rolls, halved

SLOW COOKER DIRECTIONS

1. Combine beef, barbecue sauce and 1½ cups water in slow cooker. Cover; cook on LOW 2 hours.

2. To serve, shred beef with 2 forks; place on rolls.

Makes 10 to 12 sandwiches

Tip: Use chopped deli roast beef for cooked beef. Or, substitute a 3- to 4-pound boneless beef chuck shoulder roast for cooked beef. Do not add water. Cook on LOW 8 to 10 hours.

Steak Au Jus

1 (2-pound) boneless sirloin steak
1 envelope LIPTON® RECIPE SECRETS® Onion
**   Soup Mix***
2 tablespoons BERTOLLI® Olive Oil
½ cup hot water

*Also terrific with LIPTON® RECIPE SECRETS® Savory Herb with Garlic, Ranch, Onion Mushroom or Beefy Onion Soup Mix.

1. In broiler pan, without the rack, arrange steak. Brush both sides of steak with soup mix blended with oil.

2. Broil steak until desired doneness, turning once.

3. Remove steak to serving platter. Add hot water to pan and stir, scraping brown bits from bottom of pan. Serve sauce over steak. *Makes 6 servings*

Prep Time: 5 minutes
Cook Time: 18 minutes

Beef & Pork

1-2-3 Chili

2 pounds ground beef
3 cans (15½ ounces each) chili beans in mild
**   or spicy sauce, undrained**
4 cans (8 ounces each) tomato sauce

SLOW COOKER DIRECTIONS

1. Brown beef in large nonstick skillet over medium-high heat, stirring to break up meat. Drain fat. Combine beef, beans and tomato sauce in slow cooker; mix well.

2. Cover; cook on LOW 6 to 8 hours. Serve with desired toppings.   *Makes 8 servings*

Mustard-Crusted Pork Roast

1 boneless pork loin roast, about 2 pounds
2 tablespoons spicy mustard
1 cup garlic croutons, crushed*

*Place croutons in plastic bag; roll with rolling pin until crushed.

Heat oven to 400°F. Season roast with salt and pepper; place in shallow pan and roast for 30 minutes. Remove from oven; spread surface with mustard and sprinkle with crouton crumbs. Return to oven and continue to roast for 10 to 15 minutes longer, until meat thermometer registers 155°F.

Makes 4 to 6 servings

Favorite recipe from *National Pork Board*

Glazed Pork Loin

1 bag (1 pound) baby carrots
4 boneless pork loin chops
1 jar (8 ounces) apricot preserves

SLOW COOKER DIRECTIONS

1. Place carrots on bottom of slow cooker. Place pork on carrots; spread with preserves.

2. Cover; cook on LOW 8 hours or on HIGH 4 hours.

Makes 4 servings

Super-Easy Beef Burritos

1 boneless beef chuck roast (2 to 3 pounds)
1 can (28 ounces) enchilada sauce
4 (8-inch) flour tortillas

SLOW COOKER DIRECTIONS

1. Place roast in slow cooker; cover with enchilada sauce. Add 2 to 3 tablespoons water, if desired.

2. Cover; cook on LOW 6 to 8 hours or until beef begins to fall apart. Shred beef; serve with tortillas. *Makes 4 servings*

Honey Ham
and Whipped Sweet Potatoes

Whipped Sweet Potatoes (recipe follows)
2 tablespoons mustard
2 tablespoons honey
2 ham steaks (8 ounces each)

MICROWAVE DIRECTIONS

1. Prepare Whipped Sweet Potatoes.

2. Combine mustard and honey in small cup. Place ham steaks in small microwavable baking dish; brush with mustard mixture. Microwave on MEDIUM-HIGH (70%) 1 minute or until hot.

3. Cut each steak in half to serve. Serve with sweet potatoes.

Makes 4 servings

Whipped Sweet Potatoes

2 large sweet potatoes (about 2 pounds)
2 tablespoons butter
2 tablespoons apple jelly
½ teaspoon salt

MICROWAVE DIRECTIONS

1. Pierce potatoes in several places with fork. Microwave on HIGH 10 minutes. Turn potatoes over; microwave 5 minutes more or until tender. Let stand 2 minutes; peel.

2. Place potatoes in medium bowl. Add butter, apple jelly and salt. Mash with potato masher or fork until smooth. Whip with whisk until light and fluffy.

Makes 4 servings

Apricot-Mustard Grilled Pork Tenderloin

1 pork tenderloin (about 1 pound)
5 tablespoons honey mustard
3 tablespoons apricot preserves

Season tenderloin with salt and pepper. In small bowl, stir together mustard and preserves. Grill pork over a medium-hot fire, brushing with mustard mixture frequently, turning once or twice until just done, about 15 minutes.   *Makes 4 servings*

Favorite recipe from *National Pork Board*

Sizzlin' Burgers

1 pound ground beef
¼ cup *French's*® Worcestershire Sauce
½ teaspoon garlic salt

1. Combine ground beef, Worcestershire and garlic salt; shape into 4 burgers.

2. Grill over medium heat for 15 minutes or until no longer pink in center, turning once.

3. Serve burgers on rolls. Splash on more Worcestershire to taste.   *Makes 4 servings*

Prep Time: 5 minutes
Cook Time: 15 minutes

Autumn Delight

4 to 6 beef cubed steaks
2 cans (10¾ ounces each) condensed
cream of mushroom soup, undiluted
1 package (1 ounce) dry onion soup mix
or mushroom soup mix

SLOW COOKER DIRECTIONS

1. Lightly brown cubed steaks in oil in large nonstick skillet over medium heat. Place steaks in slow cooker.

2. Combine soup, 1 cup water and dry soup mix in large bowl; blend well. Pour over steaks. Cover; cook on LOW 4 to 6 hours.

Makes 4 to 6 servings

Hash-Stuffed Potatoes

4 large baking potatoes (10 to 12 ounces each)
1 can (15 ounces) corned beef hash
4 eggs

1. Preheat oven to 350°F.

2. Cut thin slice from top of each potato. Using melon baller, scoop out insides of each potato, leaving a ½-inch-thick shell. Fill each potato with about ½ cup of corned beef hash.

3. Place filled potatoes on lightly greased baking sheet. Bake 55 minutes or until tender when pierced with fork.

4. Prepare eggs as desired. Serve on top of potatoes.

Makes 4 servings

Poultry & Seafood

Louisiana Hot and Spicy Shrimp

**1 ½ pounds uncooked medium shrimp, peeled and
deveined
1 cup LAWRY'S® Louisiana Red Pepper Marinade
With Lemon Juice
Wooden skewers, soaked in water for
15 minutes**

In large resealable plastic bag, combine shrimp and ¾ cup
Louisiana Red Pepper Marinade; turn to coat. Close bag and
marinate in refrigerator for 30 minutes. Remove shrimp from
Marinade, discard Marinade.

On wooden skewers, thread shrimp. Grill, brushing with
remaining ¼ cup Marinade, until shrimp turn pink.

Makes 6 servings

Prep Time: 10 minutes
Marinate Time: 30 minutes
Cook Time: 6 minutes

Grilled Garlic Chicken

**1 envelope LIPTON® RECIPE SECRETS® Savory
  Herb with Garlic Soup Mix
3 tablespoons BERTOLLI® Olive Oil
4 boneless, skinless chicken breast halves
  (about 1¼ pounds)**

1. In medium bowl, combine soup mix with oil.

2. Add chicken; toss to coat.

3. Grill or broil until chicken is thoroughly cooked.

Makes 4 servings

Baked Chicken

**1 chicken (4 to 5 pounds) cut into pieces,
  skin removed
1 cup buttermilk**

1. Sprinkle chicken with ¼ teaspoon each salt and pepper.
Place chicken in large resealable food storage bag. Add
buttermilk; seal bag. Marinate in refrigerator at least 1 hour.

2. Preheat oven to 350°F. Lightly spray 13×9-inch baking dish
with nonstick cooking spray.

3. Remove chicken from bag; discard buttermilk. Arrange
chicken in single layer in prepared dish. Cover dish with foil.
Bake 35 to 45 minutes. Remove foil; bake 20 minutes more or
until chicken is cooked through and juices run clear.

Makes 6 servings

Tip: *Removing skin from chicken reduces the fat. The meat remains
tender and juicy even without the skin because it is cooked covered.*

Sweet & Crispy Oven-Baked Chicken

1 pound boneless skinless chicken breast halves
¼ cup *French's*® Honey Mustard
1⅓ cups crushed *French's*® French Fried Onions

1. Coat chicken with mustard. Dip into French Fried Onions. Place into lightly greased baking pan.

2. Bake at 400°F for 20 minutes or until no longer pink in center. *Makes 4 servings*

Prep Time: 5 minutes
Cook Time: 20 minutes

Grilled Chicken Sandwiches

¾ cup WISH-BONE® Italian Dressing
6 boneless, skinless chicken breast halves
**   (about 1½ pounds)**
6 rolls

1. In large, shallow nonaluminum baking dish or plastic bag, pour ½ cup Wish-Bone Italian Dressing over chicken. Cover, or close bag, and marinate in refrigerator, turning once, up to 3 hours.

2. Remove chicken, discarding marinade. Grill or broil chicken, turning once and brushing frequently with remaining Dressing, until chicken is thoroughly cooked. Serve on rolls and garnish, if desired, with lettuce. *Makes 6 servings*

Prep Time: 5 Minutes
Marinate Time: 30 Minutes
Cook Time: 10 Minutes

Magically Moist Chicken

4 boneless, skinless chicken breast halves (about 1¼ pounds)
½ cup HELLMANN'S® or BEST FOODS® Real Mayonnaise
1¼ cups Italian seasoned dry bread crumbs

1. Preheat oven to 425°F.

2. Brush chicken with Hellmann's or Best Foods Real Mayonnaise, then coat with bread crumbs. On baking pan arrange chicken.

3. Bake 20 minutes or until chicken is thoroughly cooked.

Makes 4 servings

Variation: Also terrific with Hellmann's or Best Foods Light Mayonnaise or Hellmann's or Best Foods Canola Real Mayonnaise.

Prep Time: 5 minutes
Cook Time: 20 minutes

The Original Ranch® Crispy Chicken

¼ cup unseasoned bread crumbs or corn flake crumbs
1 packet (1 ounce) HIDDEN VALLEY® The Original Ranch® Salad Dressing & Seasoning Mix
6 bone-in chicken pieces

Combine bread crumbs and salad dressing & seasoning mix in a resealable plastic bag. Add chicken pieces; seal bag. Shake to coat chicken. Bake chicken on an ungreased baking sheet at 375°F for 50 minutes or until no longer pink in center and juices run clear.

Makes 4 to 6 servings

Crispy Onion Chicken Fingers

1⅓ cups *French's*® French Fried Onions
1 pound boneless skinless chicken fingers
3 to 4 tablespoons *French's*® Honey Mustard

1. Preheat oven to 400°F. Place French Fried Onions in resealable plastic food storage bag; seal. Crush onions with rolling pin.

2. Coat chicken fingers with mustard. Dip into crushed onions. Place chicken on baking sheet.

3. Bake 15 minutes or until chicken is crispy and no longer pink in center. *Makes 4 servings*

Prep Time: 10 minutes
Cook Time: 15 minutes

Cherry Glazed Turkey Breast

1 bone-in (2½-pound) turkey breast half
½ cup cherry preserves
1 tablespoon red wine vinegar

Prepare grill for indirect-heat cooking. Place turkey, skin side up, on rack over drip pan. Cover and grill turkey breast 1 to 1¼ hours or until meat thermometer inserted in thickest portion of breast registers 170°F.

Combine preserves and vinegar in small bowl. Brush glaze on breast ½ hour before end of grilling time. Remove turkey breast from grill and let stand 15 minutes.

To serve, slice breast and arrange on platter. *Makes 6 servings*

Favorite recipe from *National Turkey Federation*

Country Herb Roasted Chicken

**1 chicken (2½ to 3 pounds), cut into serving
pieces (with or without skin) *or* 1½ pounds
boneless skinless chicken breast halves**
**1 envelope LIPTON® RECIPE SECRETS® Savory Herb
with Garlic Soup Mix**
2 tablespoons water
1 tablespoon BERTOLLI® Olive Oil

1. Preheat oven to 375°F.

2. In 13×9-inch baking or roasting pan, arrange chicken.
In small bowl, combine remaining ingredients; brush onto
chicken.

3. For chicken pieces, bake uncovered 45 minutes or until
chicken is thoroughly cooked. For chicken breast halves, bake
uncovered 20 minutes or until chicken is thoroughly cooked.

Makes about 4 servings

Baked Salmon

4 salmon fillets
4 teaspoons fresh lemon juice
2 teaspoons Cajun seasoning mix

1. Preheat oven to 325°F.

2. Rinse salmon; pat dry. Place each fillet in center of
large triangle of parchment paper on baking sheet. Sprinkle
fillets with lemon juice and seasoning.

3. Double fold sides and ends of parchment paper to form
packets, leaving head space for heat circulation. Bake 20 to
25 minutes. Carefully open packets to allow steam to escape.
Salmon is done when it flakes easily with fork.

Makes 4 servings

Hot & Sour Chicken

**4 to 6 boneless skinless chicken breasts
(about 1 to 1½ pounds)
1 cup chicken or vegetable broth
1 package (1 ounce) dry hot-and-sour soup mix**

SLOW COOKER DIRECTIONS

1. Place chicken in slow cooker. Add broth and soup mix.

2. Cover; cook on LOW 5 to 6 hours.   *Makes 4 to 6 servings*

Magic Grilled Turkey Burgers

**1 pound ground turkey
4 teaspoons water
4 teaspoons Chef Paul Prudhomme's
Poultry Magic®, divided***

**Any of Chef Paul's Magic Seasoning Blends® will work well in this recipe. If
you prefer a less seasoned dish, simply cut back the amount of Poultry Magic®
that you use.*

Combine meat, water and 2 teaspoons Poultry Magic® and fold
in gently. Shape mixture into 4 patties, about 4 ounces each.
Season patties evenly on both sides with remaining 2 teaspoons
of Poultry Magic®. Place patties on grill and cook, turning
several times, until patties are nicely browned on both sides
and cooked through. (At least 160°F in center. Use meat
thermometer to be sure they are fully cooked.)

Serve immediately with all your favorite hamburger fixings.
                                        Makes 4 servings

Grilled Tequila Lime Salmon

**1 cup LAWRY'S® Tequila Lime Marinade
with Lime Juice
4 salmon steaks**

In large resealable plastic bag, pour ¾ cup Tequila Lime
Marinade with Lime Juice over salmon; turn to coat. Close
bag and marinate in refrigerator 30 minutes.

Remove salmon from Marinade, discarding Marinade. Grill
or broil salmon, turning once and brushing frequently with
remaining ¼ cup Marinade, 8 minutes or until fish flakes
with fork.   *Makes 4 servings*

Honey BBQ Chicken

**3 to 4 pounds bone-in chicken pieces
1 cup *Cattlemen's®* Golden Honey Barbecue Sauce**

1. Grill chicken over medium direct heat for 45 minutes
(or in a 375°F oven).

2. Baste with barbecue sauce. Cook 15 minutes longer until
no longer pink near bone. Serve with additional sauce on the
side.   *Makes 4 to 6 servings*

Fiesta Chicken

**4 boneless skinless chicken breasts
1 jar (32 ounces) chunky salsa
1 onion or green bell pepper, chopped**

SLOW COOKER DIRECTIONS

1. Place all ingredients in slow cooker.

2. Cover; cook on LOW 4 to 6 hours.   *Makes 4 servings*

Spicy Shredded Chicken

**6 boneless skinless chicken breasts
(about 1½ pounds)
1 jar (16 ounces) salsa**

SLOW COOKER DIRECTIONS

1. Place chicken in slow cooker. Cover with salsa.

2. Cover; cook on LOW 6 to 8 hours or until chicken is tender. Shred chicken with two forks before serving. *Makes 6 servings*

E-Z Lemon 'n' Herb Roasted Chicken

**1 whole fryer chicken (3½ to 4 pounds)
1 large SUNKIST® lemon, cut in half
Fresh rosemary and/or thyme sprigs**

For easy clean-up, line a 13×9×2-inch baking pan with aluminum foil. Spray a small roasting rack with nonstick cooking spray and place in baking pan. Remove neck and giblets from body cavity of chicken, and remove any excess fat; cut off tail. Rinse chicken well and pat dry with paper toweling. Place breast-side up on rack. Turn wing tips under back of chicken. With fingers, carefully separate skin from breast meat, starting at back and working towards neck end. Squeeze juice of ½ lemon; pour some under separated skin and remainder over top of breast, legs and wings. Cut remaining ½ lemon into 4 or 6 wedges and place in body cavity of chicken along with several herb sprigs. (It is not necessary to close body cavity with skewers or tie legs together.) Roast, uncovered, at 375°F. for 1¼ to 1½ hours until juices run clear when chicken is pierced in thickest part of thigh or internal temperature of thigh reaches 180°F., basting occasionally with pan drippings. Let stand 15 to 20 minutes before carving. To serve, arrange a few fresh herb sprigs at cavity opening. Garnish with lemon wedges, if desired.
Makes 4 to 5 servings

Simple Sides

Green Onion-Herb Crescent Rolls

1 package (8 ounces) refrigerated crescent roll dough
3 tablespoons minced green onions (both white and green parts)
½ teaspoon dried Italian seasoning

1. Preheat oven to 375°F. Separate dough into 8 triangles. Sprinkle about 1 teaspoon green onions over each triangle. Roll up loosely, starting at wide end of each triangle, to opposite point.

2. Place rolls on ungreased baking sheet; curve each into crescent shape. Sprinkle with Italian seasoning. Bake 10 to 12 minutes or until golden brown. *Makes 8 servings*

Variation: Other herbs and spices such as chopped parsley, black pepper and sesame seeds can be used in place of the Italian seasoning.

Prep Time: 10 minutes
Bake Time: 10 minutes

Cheddar Baked Potatoes

1 jar (1 pound) RAGÚ® Cheesy! Double Cheddar Sauce
1 bag (16 ounces) frozen vegetables, cooked and drained
6 large baking potatoes, unpeeled and baked

In 2-quart saucepan, heat Sauce. Stir in vegetables; heat through.

Cut a lengthwise slice from top of each potato. Lightly mash pulp in each potato. Evenly spoon sauce mixture onto each potato. Sprinkle, if desired, with ground black pepper.

Makes 6 servings

Prep Time: 20 minutes
Cook Time: 10 minutes

Party Sprouts

1 pound Brussels sprouts
1 cup chicken broth
1 red bell pepper, diced

1. Trim Brussels sprouts. Cut an X in stem ends. Bring broth to a boil in large skillet over high heat. Add Brussels sprouts; return to boil. Reduce heat to medium-low. Simmer, covered, 5 minutes.

2. Stir in bell pepper. Simmer, covered, 5 minutes or until Brussels sprouts are just tender. Drain before serving.

Makes 4 servings

String Cheese Spaghetti

1 box (16 ounces) spaghetti, cooked and drained
1 jar (1 pound 10 ounces) RAGÚ® Organic Pasta Sauce, heated
2 cups diced mozzarella cheese (about 8 ounces)

In large serving bowl, toss all ingredients. Garnish, if desired, with grated Parmesan cheese and chopped fresh parsley.

Makes 6 servings

Prep Time: 20 minutes

Chutney'd Squash Circles

2 acorn squash (1 pound each)
2 tablespoons butter or margarine
¹/₂ cup prepared chutney

1. Preheat oven to 400°F. Slice tip and stem end from squash. Cut squash crosswise into ³/₄-inch rings. Scoop out and discard seeds.

2. Tear off 18-inch square of heavy-duty foil. Center foil in 13×9-inch baking dish. Dot foil with butter; place squash on butter, slightly overlapping rings. Spoon chutney over slices; sprinkle with 2 tablespoons water.

3. Bring foil on long sides of pan together in center, folding over to make tight seam. Fold ends to form tight seal.

4. Bake 20 to 30 minutes until squash is fork-tender. Transfer to warm serving plate. Pour pan drippings over squash.

Makes 4 servings

Oven-Roasted Asparagus

1 bunch (12 to 14 ounces) asparagus spears
1 tablespoon olive oil
¼ cup shredded Asiago or Parmesan cheese

1. Preheat oven to 425°F.

2. Trim off and discard tough ends of asparagus spears. Peel stem ends with vegetable peeler, if desired. Arrange asparagus in shallow baking dish. Drizzle oil over asparagus; turn spears to coat. Sprinkle with salt and pepper.

3. Roast asparagus until tender, about 12 to 18 minutes depending on thickness of asparagus. Chop or leave spears whole. Sprinkle with cheese.   *Makes 4 servings*

Herbed Corn on the Cob

1 tablespoon butter or margarine
1 teaspoon mixed dried herb leaves (such as basil, oregano, sage and rosemary)
4 ears corn, husks removed

MICROWAVE DIRECTIONS

1. Combine butter, herbs, ¼ teaspoon salt and ⅛ teaspoon pepper in small microwavable bowl. Microwave on MEDIUM (50%) 30 to 45 seconds or until butter is melted.

2. With pastry brush, coat corn with butter mixture. Place corn on microwavable plate; microwave on HIGH 5 to 6 minutes. Turn corn over; microwave on HIGH 5 to 6 minutes or until tender.   *Makes 4 servings*

Original Ranch® & Cheddar Bread

**2 cups (8 ounces) shredded sharp Cheddar
cheese**
**1 cup HIDDEN VALLEY® The Original Ranch®
Salad Dressing**
**1 whole loaf (1 pound) French bread (not sour
dough)**

Combine cheese and salad dressing in a medium bowl. Cut
bread in half lengthwise. Place on a broiler pan and spread
dressing mixture evenly over cut side of each half. Broil until
lightly brown. Cut each half into 8 pieces.   *Makes 16 pieces*

Crispy Onion Crescent Rolls

1 can (8 ounces) refrigerated crescent dinner rolls
**1⅓ cups *French's*® French Fried Onions, slightly
crushed**
1 egg, beaten

Preheat oven to 375°F. Line large baking sheet with foil.
Separate refrigerated rolls into 8 triangles. Sprinkle center of
each triangle with about 1½ tablespoons French Fried Onions.
Roll up triangles from short side, jelly-roll fashion. Sprinkle any
excess onions over top of crescents.

Arrange crescents on prepared baking sheet. Brush with beaten
egg. Bake 15 minutes or until golden brown and crispy. Transfer
to wire rack; cool slightly.   *Makes 8 servings*

Prep Time: 15 minutes
Cook Time: 15 minutes

Cauliflower Mashed "Potatoes"

2 heads cauliflower (to equal 8 cups florets)
1 tablespoon butter
1 tablespoon half-and-half, cream, whole milk,
buttermilk or chicken broth

1. Break cauliflower into equal-size florets. Place in large saucepan in about 2 inches of water. Simmer over medium heat 20 to 25 minutes, or until cauliflower is very tender and falling apart. (Check occasionally to make sure there is enough water to prevent burning; add water if necessary.) Drain well.

2. Place cooked cauliflower in food processor or blender. Process until almost smooth. Add butter. Process until smooth, adding cream as needed to reach desired consistency. Season with salt. *Makes 6 servings*

Honey-Glazed Carrots and Parsnips

½ pound carrots, thinly sliced
½ pound parsnips, peeled and thinly sliced
2 tablespoons honey

1. Steam carrots and parsnips over simmering water in large saucepan 3 to 4 minutes or until crisp-tender. Rinse under cold running water; drain. Combine carrots, parsnips and honey in same saucepan.

2. Cook over medium heat just until heated through. Serve immediately. *Makes 6 servings*

Sweet & Tangy Coleslaw

1 small bag (16 ounces) shredded cabbage
½ cup mayonnaise
½ cup *French's*® Honey Mustard

1. Combine ingredients in large bowl until blended.

2. Chill until ready to serve. *Makes 6 to 8 servings*

Prep Time: 5 minutes

Herbed Green Beans

1 pound fresh green beans, ends removed
1 teaspoon extra-virgin olive oil
2 tablespoons chopped fresh basil
**   *or* 2 teaspoons dried basil**

1. Steam green beans 5 minutes or until crisp-tender. Rinse under cold running water; drain and set aside.

2. Just before serving, heat oil in large nonstick skillet over medium-low heat. Add basil; cook and stir 1 minute. Add green beans; cook until heated through. Garnish with additional fresh basil, if desired. Serve immediately. *Makes 6 servings*

Tip:

When buying green beans, look for vivid green, crisp beans without scars. Pods should be well shaped and slim with small seeds. Buy beans of uniform size to ensure even cooking and avoid bruised or large beans.

Onion-Roasted Potatoes

**1 envelope LIPTON® RECIPE SECRETS® Onion
  Soup Mix***
**4 medium all-purpose potatoes, cut into large
  chunks (about 2 pounds)**
⅓ cup BERTOLLI® Olive Oil

**Also terrific with LIPTON® RECIPE SECRETS® Onion Mushroom, Golden
Onion or Savory Herb with Garlic Soup Mix.*

1. Preheat oven to 450°F. In 13×9-inch baking or roasting pan,
combine all ingredients.

2. Bake uncovered, stirring occasionally, 40 minutes or until
potatoes are tender and golden brown.   *Makes 4 servings*

Prep Time: 10 minutes
Cook Time: 40 minutes

Grilled Asparagus

1 pound asparagus, washed and trimmed
2 tablespoons olive oil
1 tablespoon MRS. DASH® Original Blend

Place asparagus in large bowl, drizzle with olive oil and
sprinkle with Mrs. Dash® Original Blend to taste. Toss to coat
evenly.

Place asparagus in grilling basket. Grill over medium-high heat
8 minutes, turning periodically, until asparagus is fork-tender.
                                        Makes 4 servings

Prep Time: 5 minutes
Cook Time: 8 minutes

70   Onion-Roasted Potatoes

Simple Sides

Smoky Kale Chiffonade

¾ pound fresh young kale or mustard greens
3 slices bacon
2 tablespoons crumbled blue cheese

1. Rinse kale well in large bowl of warm water; place in colander. Drain. Discard any discolored leaves and trim away tough stem ends.

2. To prepare chiffonade, roll up leaves jelly-roll fashion. Slice crosswise into ¹/₂-inch-thick slices; separate into strips. Set aside.

3. Cook bacon in large skillet over medium heat until crisp. Remove bacon to paper towel. Remove all but 1 tablespoon drippings.

4. Add reserved kale to drippings in skillet. Cook and stir over medium-high heat 2 to 3 minutes until wilted and tender (older leaves may take slightly longer).*

5. Crumble bacon. Toss bacon and blue cheese with kale. Transfer to warm serving dish. Serve immediately.

Makes 4 servings

*If using mustard greens, stir-fry 4 to 6 minutes until wilted and tender.

Note: *"Chiffonade" in French literally means "made of rags." In cooking, it means "cut into thin strips."*

Original Ranch® Mashed Potatoes

4 cups hot unsalted mashed potatoes (with or without skins)
1 packet (1 ounce) HIDDEN VALLEY® The Original Ranch® Salad Dressing & Seasoning Mix
Butter or margarine (optional)

Combine potatoes and salad dressing & seasoning mix; stir well. Serve with butter or margarine, if desired.

Makes 4 servings

Salsa Macaroni & Cheese

1 jar (1 pound) RAGÚ® Cheesy! Double Cheddar Sauce
1 cup prepared mild salsa
8 ounces elbow macaroni, cooked and drained

1. In 2-quart saucepan, heat Double Cheddar Sauce over medium heat. Stir in salsa; heat through.

2. Toss with hot macaroni. Serve immediately.

Makes 4 servings

Prep Time: 5 minutes
Cook Time: 15 minutes

Green Beans with Pine Nuts

1 pound green beans, trimmed
2 tablespoons butter or margarine
2 tablespoons pine nuts

1. Cook beans in 1 inch water in covered 3-quart saucepan 6 to 8 minutes or until crisp-tender; drain.

2. Melt butter in large skillet over medium heat. Add pine nuts; cook, stirring frequently, until golden. Add beans; stir gently to coat beans with butter. Season with salt and pepper.

Makes 4 servings

Lots
of Sweets

Glazed Donut Cookies

1 package (18 ounces) refrigerated oatmeal raisin cookie dough in squares or rounds (12 count)
Prepared white or chocolate frosting
Assorted colored sprinkles

1. Preheat oven to 350°F. Grease 12 ($2^{1}/_{2}$- or $2^{3}/_{4}$-inch) muffin pan cups.

2. Remove dough from wrapper. Separate dough into 12 pieces; let stand at room temperature about 15 minutes.

3. Shape each dough piece into 12-inch-long rope on lightly floured surface. Coil ropes into muffin cups, leaving centers open.

4. Bake 12 minutes; remove from oven and re-shape center hole with round handle of wooden spoon. Return to oven; bake 3 to 4 minutes or until set.

5. Remove from oven; re-shape holes, if necessary. Cool in pan 4 minutes; transfer cookies to wire racks to cool completely.

6. Spread frosting over cookies; decorate with sprinkles.

Makes 12 large cookies

Black & White Bars

1 package (18 ounces) refrigerated sugar cookie dough
1 package (18 ounces) refrigerated triple chocolate cookie dough
2 squares (1 ounce each) white chocolate, finely chopped

1. Lightly grease 11×7-inch baking pan. Let both packages of dough stand at room temperature about 15 minutes.

2. Preheat oven to 350°F. Press sugar cookie dough evenly onto bottom of prepared pan. Freeze 15 minutes.

3. Press triple chocolate dough evenly over sugar dough in pan. Bake 37 to 40 minutes or until edges are brown and center is set. Cool completely in pan on wire rack.

4. Place white chocolate in small resealable food storage bag. Microwave on MEDIUM (50%) 1 minute; knead bag lightly. Microwave and knead at additional 30-second intervals until white chocolate is completely melted. Cut off tiny corner of bag. Drizzle white chocolate over bars. Let stand until set.

Makes 1 dozen bars

Pineapple Dessert

1 container (8 ounces) whipped cream cheese
1 can (14 ounces) sweetened condensed milk
3 cans (20 ounces each) pineapple chunks or fruit cocktail, drained

1. Beat cream cheese and condensed milk in large bowl with electric mixer. Add pineapple chunks; beat well.

2. Cover; chill in refrigerator overnight.

Makes 6 to 8 servings

Peanut Butter & Jelly Pockets

1 package (18 ounces) refrigerated peanut butter cookie dough
1 jar (10 ounces) strawberry or raspberry pastry filling
Coarse decorating sugar

1. Freeze dough 1 hour or until completely firm.

2. Preheat oven to 350°F. Lightly grease cookie sheets.

3. Cut dough into ¼-inch slices; place half of dough slices 2 inches apart on prepared cookie sheets. Spoon about 1 teaspoon pastry filling each onto centers of dough slices; top with remaining dough slices. Sprinkle tops with decorating sugar.

4. Bake 12 to 15 minutes or until edges are light brown. Cool on cookie sheets 3 minutes. Remove to wire racks; cool completely. *Makes about 1½ dozen cookies*

Mango-Peach Frozen Yogurt

2 medium (8 ounces each) ripe mangoes, peeled and cubed
2 cups peach low-fat yogurt
½ cup honey

In blender or food processor container, process mango cubes until smooth. Add yogurt and honey; process until well combined. Transfer mixture to ice cream maker; freeze according to manufacturer's directions. *Makes 6 servings*

Favorite recipe from **National Honey Board**

Milk Chocolate Pots de Crème

2 cups (11½-ounce package) HERSHEY'S Milk Chocolate Chips
½ cup light cream
½ teaspoon vanilla extract

1. Place milk chocolate chips and light cream in medium microwave-safe bowl. Microwave at HIGH (100%) 1 minute or just until chips are melted and mixture is smooth when stirred. Stir in vanilla.

2. Pour into demitasse cups or very small dessert dishes. Cover; refrigerate until firm. Serve cold with sweetened whipped cream, if desired. *Makes 6 to 8 servings*

Peanut Butter and Milk Chocolate Chip Mudd Balls

1 cup HERSHEY'S® Milk Chocolate Chips, divided
1 cup REESE'S® Peanut Butter Chips, divided
½ teaspoon shortening (do not use butter, margarine, spread or oil)

1. Stir together milk chocolate chips and peanut butter chips. Coarsely chop 1⅓ cups chip mixture in food processor or by hand; place in medium bowl.

2. Place remaining ⅔ cup chip mixture and shortening in small microwave-safe bowl. Microwave at HIGH (100%) 45 seconds; stir. If necessary, microwave at HIGH an additional 15 seconds at a time, stirring after each heating, until chips are melted and mixture is smooth.

3. Pour melted chocolate mixture over chopped chips; stir to coat evenly. With hands, form mixture into 1-inch balls. Place in small candy cups, if desired. Store in cool, dry place. *Makes about 20 pieces*

Chocolate Peanut Butter Ice Cream Sandwiches

2 tablespoons creamy peanut butter
8 chocolate wafer cookies
⅔ cup vanilla ice cream, softened

1. Spread peanut butter over flat sides of all cookies.

2. Spoon ice cream over peanut butter on 4 cookies. Top with remaining 4 cookies, peanut butter sides down. Press down lightly to force ice cream to edges of sandwiches.

3. Wrap each sandwich tightly in foil. Freeze at least 2 hours or up to 5 days. *Makes 4 servings*

Chocolate-Dipped Strawberries

2 cups (11½ ounces) milk chocolate chips
1 tablespoon shortening
12 large strawberries with stems, rinsed and dried (about)

1. Line baking sheet with waxed paper; set aside.

2. Melt chips with shortening in top of double boiler over hot, not boiling, water, stirring constantly.

3. Dip about half of each strawberry in chocolate. Remove excess chocolate by scraping bottom of strawberry across rim of pan. Place strawberries on prepared baking sheet. Let stand until set.

4. Store in refrigerator in container between layers of waxed paper. *Makes about 12 strawberries*

Variation: *Melt 8 ounces white chocolate or pastel confectionery coating. Redip dipped strawberries; leave a portion of the milk chocolate coating showing.*

Hint: *Stir chopped dried fruits, raisins or nuts into any remaining chocolate; drop by tablespoonfuls onto a baking sheet lined with waxed paper.*

Chocolate Peanut Butter Ice Cream Sandwiches

Double Peanut Clusters

1⅔ cups (10-ounce package) REESE'S® Peanut
   Butter Chips
1 tablespoon shortening (do not use butter,
   margarine, spread or oil)
2 cups salted peanuts

1. Line cookie sheet with wax paper.

2. Place peanut butter chips and shortening in large microwave-safe bowl. Microwave at HIGH (100%) 1½ minutes; stir until chips are melted and mixture is smooth. If necessary, microwave an additional 30 seconds until chips are melted when stirred. Stir in peanuts.

3. Drop by rounded teaspoons onto prepared cookie sheet. (Mixture may also be dropped into small paper candy cups.) Cool until set. Store in cool, dry place.

Makes about 2½ dozen clusters

Butterscotch Nut Clusters: *Follow above directions, substituting 1¾ cups (11-ounce package) HERSHEY'S Butterscotch Chips for Peanut Butter Chips.*

Easy Homemade
Chocolate Ice Cream

1 (14-ounce) can EAGLE BRAND® Sweetened
   Condensed Milk (NOT evaporated milk)
⅔ cup chocolate-flavored syrup
2 cups (1 pint) whipping cream, whipped
   (do not use non-dairy whipped topping)

1. In large bowl, combine EAGLE BRAND® and chocolate syrup. Fold in whipped cream. Pour into 9×5-inch loaf pan or other 2-quart container; cover.

2. Freeze 6 hours or until firm. Return leftovers to freezer.

Makes about 1½ quarts ice cream

Tiger Stripes

1 package (12 ounces) semisweet chocolate chips
3 tablespoons creamy or chunky peanut butter, divided
2 (2-ounce) white chocolate baking bars

1. Line 8-inch square pan with foil; lightly grease foil. Melt semisweet chocolate and 2 tablespoons peanut butter in small saucepan over low heat; stir until melted and smooth. Pour chocolate mixture into prepared pan. Let stand 10 to 15 minutes to cool slightly.

2. Melt white chocolate and remaining 1 tablespoon peanut butter in small saucepan over low heat. Drop spoonfuls of white chocolate mixture over semisweet chocolate mixture in pan.

3. Using small metal spatula or knife, swirl chocolates to create tiger stripes. Freeze about 1 hour or until firm. Remove from pan; peel off foil. Cut or break into pieces. Refrigerate until ready to serve. *Makes about 3 dozen pieces*

Pineapple Whip

1 package (10 ounces) large marshmallows
**   or 1 package (about 10 ounces) miniature marshmallows**
1 can (20 ounces) crushed pineapple, undrained
1 cup heavy whipping cream

1. Cut large marshmallows into 4 or 5 pieces. Combine marshmallow pieces and pineapple with juice in large bowl. Chill 4 hours or overnight.

2. Beat whipping cream in medium bowl with electric mixer until stiff peaks form. Fold into pineapple mixture. Refrigerate until ready to serve. *Makes 6 to 8 servings*

Chocolate Macadamia Chippers

**1 package (18 ounces) refrigerated chocolate
chip cookie dough
3 tablespoons unsweetened cocoa powder
½ cup coarsely chopped macadamia nuts**

1. Preheat oven to 375°F. Let dough stand at room temperature
about 15 minutes.

2. Combine dough and cocoa in large bowl; beat until well
blended. (Dough may be kneaded lightly, if desired.) Stir in
nuts. Drop by heaping tablespoons 2 inches apart onto
ungreased cookie sheets.

3. Bake 9 to 11 minutes or until almost set. Transfer to wire
racks to cool completely. Dust lightly with powdered sugar,
if desired.   *Makes 2 dozen cookies*

Cherry Almond Clusters

**1 (8-ounce) package semisweet baking
chocolate, coarsely chopped
1 cup slivered almonds, toasted
1 cup dried tart cherries**

Place chocolate in microwave-safe bowl. Microwave on HIGH
(100% power) 2 minutes, stirring after 1 minute. Stir until
chocolate is completely melted. Add almonds and dried
cherries; mix until completely coated with chocolate. Drop
by teaspoons onto waxed paper. Refrigerate until firm.
                                          Makes 2 dozen candies

Note: *To toast almonds, spread almonds on ungreased baking sheet.
Bake in preheated 350°F oven 5 to 7 minutes, stirring occasionally.*

Favorite recipe from *Cherry Marketing Institute*

Toffee Chipsters

1 package (18 ounces) refrigerated sugar cookie dough
1 cup white chocolate chips
1 bag (8 ounces) chocolate-covered toffee baking bits, divided

1. Preheat oven to 350°F. Lightly grease cookie sheets. Let dough stand at room temperature about 15 minutes.

2. Combine dough, white chocolate chips and 1 cup toffee bits in large bowl; beat until well blended. Drop dough by rounded tablespoonfuls 2 inches apart onto prepared cookie sheets. Press remaining ⅓ cup toffee bits into dough mounds.

3. Bake 10 to 12 minutes or until set. Cool on cookie sheets 1 minute. Remove to wire racks; cool completely.

Makes about 2 dozen cookies

Lemon Chiffon

2 packages (4-serving size each) lemon-flavored gelatin
2 packages (4-serving size each) instant vanilla pudding and pie filling mix
1 container (8 ounces) frozen whipped topping, thawed

1. Combine gelatin and pudding mixes in 5-quart serving bowl. Add 3 cups boiling water; stir constantly until completely dissolved. Refrigerate about 1 hour or until mixture is chilled and has thickened slightly.

2. Stir in whipped topping; refrigerate at least 1 hour or until set.

Makes 12 servings

Toffee Chipsters

Acknowledgments

The publisher would like to thank the companies and organizations listed below for the use of their recipes and photographs in this publication.

ACH Food Companies, Inc.

Birds Eye Foods

Chef Paul Prudhomme's Magic Seasoning Blends®

Cherry Marketing Institute

EAGLE BRAND®

Heinz North America

The Hershey Company

The Hidden Valley® Food Products Company

The Kingsford® Products Co.

Mrs. Dash®

National Honey Board

National Pork Board

National Turkey Federation

Ortega®, A Division of B&G Foods, Inc.

Reckitt Benckiser Inc.

Reprinted with permission of Sunkist Growers, Inc. All Rights Reserved.

Unilever

Wisconsin Milk Marketing Board